North American Historical Atlases

THE CIVIL WAR AND RECONSTRUCTION: 1863-1877

North American Historical Atlases

THE CIVIL WAR AND RECONSTRUCTION: 1863-1877

Rebecca Stefoff

BENCHMARK BOOKS

MARSHALL CAVENDISH
NEW YORK

Benchmark Books
Marshall Cavendish Corporation
99 White Plains Road
Tarrytown, New York 10591

• • •

Library of Congress Cataloging-in-Publication Data
Stefoff, Rebecca, 1951-
The Civil War and Reconstruction: 1863–1877/by Rebecca Stefoff
p. cm—(North American historical atlases)
Includes bibliographical references and index.
Summary: Discusses the Civil War and Reconstruction and their effects
on the nation and on black Americans in particular.
ISBN 0-7614-1347-2
1. United States—History—Civil War, 1861–1865—Juvenile literature.
2. United States—History—Civil War, 1861–1865—Maps—Juvenile literature.
3. Reconstruction—Juvenile literature.   4. Reconstruction—Maps—Juvenile literature.
5. African Americans—History—1863–1877—Juvenile literature.
6. African Americans—History—1863–1877—Maps—Juvenile literature.
[1. United States—History—Civil War, 1861–1865.   2. United States—History—Civil War, 1861–1865—Maps.
3. Reconstruction.   4. Reconstruction—Maps.]   I. Title.
E468 .S85   2002   2001043900   973.7—dc21

• • •

Printed in Hong Kong
1 3 5 7 8 6 4 2

• • •

Book Designer: Judith Turziano
Photo Researcher: Candlepants Incorporated

• • •

CREDITS
Front Cover: George Woolworth Colton's United States of America, 1869, used with permission from the Library of Congress, Washington, D.C.
Back Cover: *Corbis*

The photographs in this book are used by permission and through the courtesy of: *Corbis*: 2, 8, 12, 22, 33, 34, 36, 37, 39;
Medford Historical Society, 7, 24; Bettmann, 13(top), 14, 21, 35, 40; Minnesota Historical Society, 17; *Pierpont Morgan Library/Art Resource NY*: 11;
Trustees of the Boston Public Library: 13(lower, left & right); *The Museum of the Confederacy, Richmond Virginia/Photography by
Katherine Wetzel*: 27; *Bridgeman Art Library*: Yale University Art Gallery, New Haven CT, 29; Private Collection, 31.

Contents

Chapter One

THE STORM RAGES ON

On January 1, 1863, President Abraham Lincoln signed the Emancipation Proclamation, which gave all slaves in the rebellious Southern states their freedom. The proclamation did not immediately liberate the African-American slaves under the control of the Confederacy, as the South called itself, but it gave them hope. In the winter of 1863, people on both sides of the conflict needed every reason for hope they could find. The Civil War between the North and the South had lasted for nearly two years, and most people realized that it was far from over.

Confederate Confidence

The Battle of Antietam in the fall of 1862 had given the North, or the Union, a taste of victory. That taste turned sour almost three months later at a huge battle near Fredericksburg, Virginia. General Ambrose Burnside planned to lead more than 100,000 blue-coated Union soldiers across the Rappahannock River on floating bridges and on to the Confederate capital at Richmond, Virginia. General Robert E. Lee's gray-clad Rebel army of 78,000 men waited on the hills along the far side of the river. On December 13, as the morning fog cleared, the Confederate army fired down at the Union Bluecoats streaming across the river and up the slope. At day's end, some 5,000 Confederate Rebels and more than twice that many Union Yankees lay dead or wounded on the snowy ground. Yet the Confederates had scored a thrilling victory, and Lee, who stood atop a hill watching the battle, said, "It is well that war is so terrible. We should grow too fond of it."

After the Union disaster at Fredericksburg, General Joseph Hooker replaced Burnside as the Northern commander. But before Hooker could launch an attack against Lee, Confederate forces struck at his army near Chancellorsville, Virginia, on May 2, 1863. The South won the battle, but its joy was dampened by the loss of much-

President Abraham Lincoln made Joseph Hooker (seated, second from right) commander of the Union's Army of the Potomac after the Union lost to the Confederacy in the Battle of Fredericksburg. However, Hooker soon lost the command. The failures and shortcomings of generals proved to be one of the Union's biggest problems during the war.

After the Battle of Chancellorsville, Confederate mapmaker Jed Hotchkiss spent three weeks mapping the battlefield while he grieved for the deaths of his chief commanding officer, Stonewall Jackson, and his best friend, another mapmaker, who had been killed in the fighting. Hotchkiss survived the war, and his maps and diary became important reference materials for historians of the conflict.

loved general Thomas "Stonewall" Jackson, who died after being shot accidentally by a soldier on his own side. The Union's harsh defeat caused Lincoln to replace Hooker with General George Meade. The North seemed to be floundering, unable to find a commander who could strike hard at its enemy. The South also had grave problems. Food shortages were causing riots across the region, and for months Union forces had **besieged** Vicksburg, Mississippi, threatening to capture this important stronghold overlooking the Mississippi River. But after Fredericksburg and Chancellorsville, Confederate confidence soared.

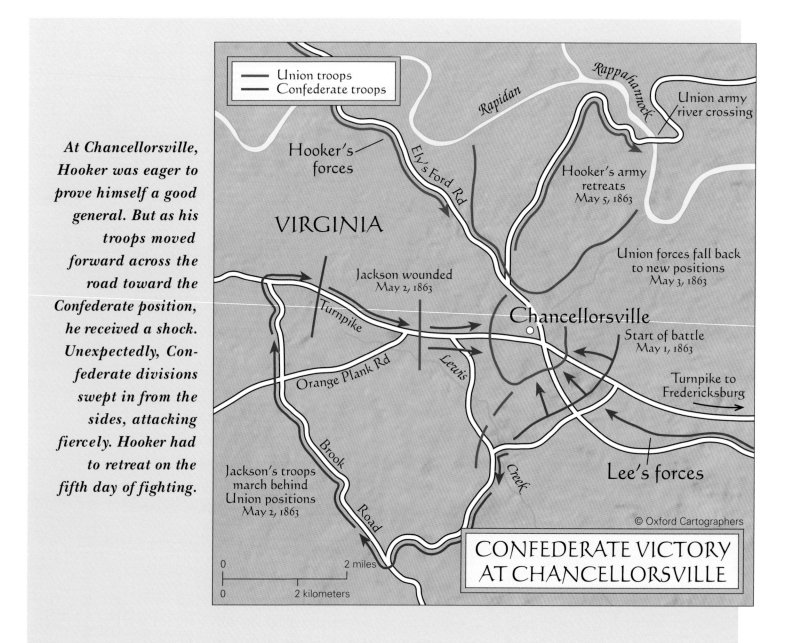

At Chancellorsville, Hooker was eager to prove himself a good general. But as his troops moved forward across the road toward the Confederate position, he received a shock. Unexpectedly, Confederate divisions swept in from the sides, attacking fiercely. Hooker had to retreat on the fifth day of fighting.

Union troops
Confederate troops

Rapidan

Rappahannock

Union army river crossing

Hooker's forces

Ely's Ford Rd

Hooker's army retreats
May 5, 1863

VIRGINIA

Union forces fall back to new positions
May 3, 1863

Jackson wounded
May 2, 1863

Turnpike

Chancellorsville

Start of battle
May 1, 1863

Orange Plank Rd

Lewis

Turnpike to Fredericksburg

Brook

Creek

Lee's forces

Jackson's troops march behind Union positions
May 2, 1863

Road

© Oxford Cartographers

0   2 miles
0   2 kilometers

CONFEDERATE VICTORY AT CHANCELLORSVILLE

At War and At Home

The Civil War affected every single American life. Divided loyalties tore families apart, especially in the slave-owning **border states** of Delaware, Maryland, Kentucky, and Missouri, which had stayed in the Union. Kentucky senator John

Crittenden, for example, saw one son became a Union general and another a Confederate general. Sometimes, though, Yankees and Rebels made temporary peace. A Union soldier told how his men and the enemy took breaks from trying to kill one another. "[O]ne of the rebels, calling a **parley**, would cry out: 'Yanks, ain't it about your time to cook coffee?' 'Yes,' replied Yank. 'Then,' rejoins Mr. Rebel, 'if you won't shoot while I make my **johnnycake**, I won't shoot while you cook your coffee.'"

Such truces were rare. Troops on both sides found the war horrific. During the fighting, gun smoke, or "fog of battle," often became so thick that it was impossible to tell friend from foe. Death came in many forms—a bullet, a cannon, the trampling hooves of a cavalry horse, or a ripping **bayonet** wound. Most soldiers hoped for a quick death, because the fate of the wounded was dreadful. An injured man could lie on the battlefield for hours in sweltering heat or bitter cold, weeping and waiting for the overworked medical teams to reach him. Despite the best efforts of doctors and nurses, thousands of soldiers survived battles only to die days or weeks later from infected wounds. Illnesses such as cholera and pneumonia also

Soldiers move wounded men from a Civil War battlefield. Each side respected the other's need to care for the injured, and sometimes after a battle Union and Confederate teams would move across the field side by side, silently gathering their fallen soldiers.

ravaged armies already weakened by poor nutrition and exhaustion. Frightened and disgusted, about a tenth of all soldiers on each side **deserted** during the war.

The war was also hard on those at home. The work of farms, stores, factories, and businesses fell to women, children, and the elderly, who also grieved for the soldiers who had died and worried about those still living. "While my husband was at the front doing active service, suffering fatigue, privations, and the many ills

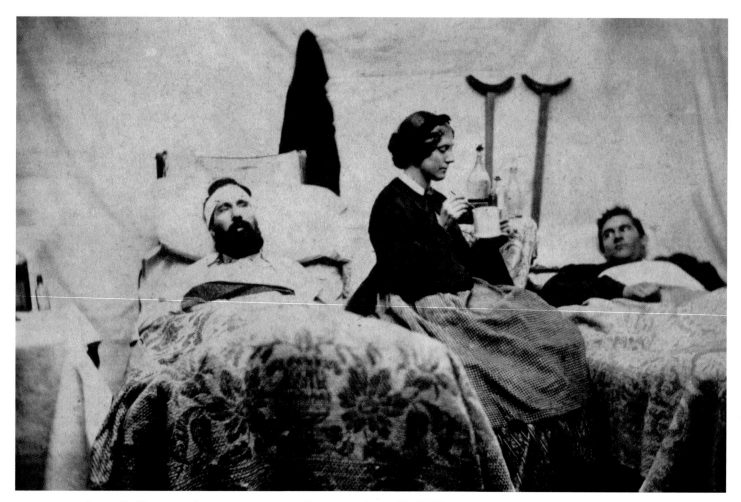

Anne Bell, one of many women who served as Civil War nurses, tends Union soldiers.

attendant on a soldier's life, I was at home struggling to keep the family comfortable," Victoria Clayton of Alabama later wrote. "Our work was hard and continuous." Many Northern and Southern women also supported the war effort with contributions of money or of supplies, such as bandages, blankets, and clothing for the troops. Hundreds of women on both sides saw service as nurses.

The Role of African Americans

As soon as the war started, black men in the North volunteered to fight. Two African Americans from Cleveland, Ohio, wrote to the U.S. war secretary, "The question now is will you allow us the poor privilege of fighting, and, if need be, dying...?" Lincoln refused to let blacks join the army, fearing that it would anger the slave states that had remained loyal

WOMEN WARRIORS

Rose Greenhow, photographed here with her daughter, spied for the Confederacy. Women on both sides of the conflict helped the cause, usually in ways other than spying. Many women struggled daily to keep farms and businesses going and to hold their families together.

At least one hundred women are known to have served as soldiers in the Civil War, disguised as men. Some of them wanted to be with the soldiers they loved, while others burned with patriotic eagerness to share the fight. Still others were driven by the spirit of adventure and the chance to escape women's traditional roles. A number of female soldiers were killed in the war. Only after their deaths did their comrades in arms discover they were women.

Other women served the Union or Confederate causes without wearing disguises. They were spies. Elizabeth Van Lew of Richmond was loyal to the Union. Together with a former slave, she gathered information about Confederate plans from the household of Confederate president Jefferson Davis and passed it on to the North. Working for the other side was Rose Greenhow of Washington, D.C., the Union capital. She smuggled information to Confederate leaders and later drowned while smuggling European gold into the Confederacy when the ship she was on was sunk by a Union gunboat.

Frances Clayton (or Clalin) of Minnesota, shown in both male and female clothing, joined the Union army along with her husband in 1861. Disguised as a man, she served until 1862, when her husband was killed and she was wounded.

A corporal in the Negro Union Infantry. The question of whether or not to allow African Americans to serve in the war troubled both North and South. In the end, the need for more soldiers forced the North to overcome its fear of allowing blacks to bear arms.

can deny that he has earned the right to citizenship," and this worried Northerners who were not ready to accept African Americans as equal citizens.

Yet African Americans quickly became an important force in the war. The Union navy, smaller than the army and less in the public view, eagerly accepted black volunteers. Escaped slaves found work as laborers in army camps. Then, in early 1863, Lincoln and the Union government allowed blacks to enlist. The Union had suffered staggering losses in battle and needed as many new soldiers as possible, and the Emancipation Proclamation had not only freed the Southern slaves but had prepared Americans to reconsider the role of free black people in society. During the second half of the war, African-American troops fought with distinction, although they served in **segregated** units and sometimes met with **prejudice** from white fellow soldiers. A total of about 200,000 African Americans served in the Union military. By the war's end, about 10 percent of the army and more than 15 percent of the navy were black.

The South also desperately needed more soldiers. Late in the war, Jefferson Davis considered letting blacks enlist. Many Southerners objected violently. One wrote, "If slaves make good soldiers, our whole theory of slavery is wrong." Davis never put the matter to the test. Although thousands of enslaved African

to the Union and drive them to the Confederate side. In addition, many people in the North resisted the idea of African-American soldiers. Black abolitionist Frederick Douglass wrote that once a black man became a soldier, "there is no power on earth which

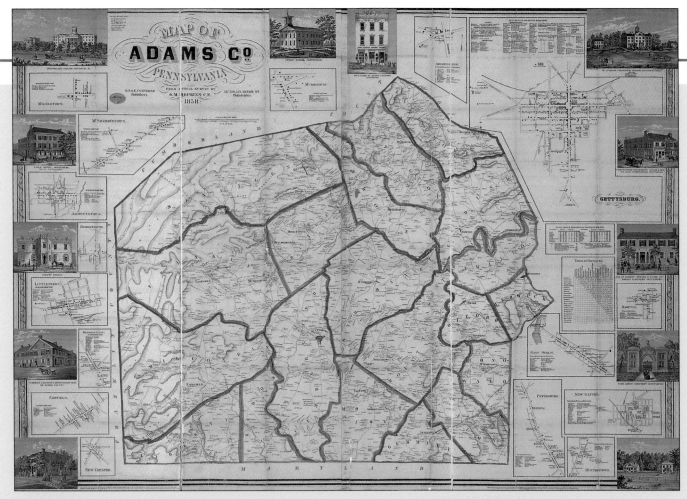

At the time of the Battle of Gettysburg, this 1858 map of Adams County, Pennsylvania, was the most detailed and accurate map of the area. Both senior commanders, Robert E. Lee of the Confederate army and George G. Meade of the Union army, had copies of it and studied them closely. The town of Gettysburg is shown in some detail because it was the county seat.

Americans supported the South with forced labor, their thoughts often turned to the freedom that awaited if the North won the war. About 10 percent of them deserted their masters, and a few aided the North with bold acts of sabotage, such as stealing a Confederate ship and turning it over to the Union navy.

Gettysburg Turns the Tide

After the Confederate victories at Fredericksburg and Chancellorsville, Lee marched a large army northward into Union territory. He hoped to terrify Northern citizens and to supply his men with Northern food, shoes, and clothing. On July 1, near Gettysburg, Pennsyl-

Chambersburg Pike

Railroad

York Pike

Lee's headquarters

Union & Confederate forces meet outside Gettysburg
July 1, 1863

Hanover Rd

Hagerstown Road

Gettysburg

Confederate troops attack Union positions at Cemetery Hill and Culp's Hill
July 2, 1863

Seminary Ridge

Confederate forces begin retreat to Virginia
July 4, 1863

Cemetery Hill

Culp's Hill

Meade's headquarters

Confederate charge fails to break the center of the Union line
July 3, 1863

Cemetery Ridge

Rock

Willoughby Run

Emmitsburg Road

Plum Run

Baltimore Pike

Creek

PENNSYLVANIA

Confederate troops drive Union forces to Cemetery Ridge and Little Round Top
July 2, 1863

Little Round Top

Taneytown Rd

| 0 | | 1 mile |
| 0 | | 1 kilometer |

Round Top

© Oxford Cartographers

—— Union troops
—— Confederate troops

BATTLE OF GETTYSBURG

At Gettysburg, Confederate troops forced Union troops onto a series of hilltops and then surrounded them on both sides. In spite of repeated attacks and charges, however, the Southerners could not break the line of Northern troops that fired down on them. One of the South's problems was that Lee could not communicate well with his various officers or get them to act together on a single shared plan. He had hoped for a major victory, but in the end he had to retreat. However, Lee's defeat was not as crushing as it would have been if Union forces had pursued and attacked his retreating army.

The Battle of Gettysburg sprawled over a much larger area than is shown in this 1905 painting. Today, the battlefield is preserved as a historic site, and visitors can walk over its rugged terrain, imagining how the battle unfolded over several hot summer days.

vania, Southern and Northern armies clashed in what became a three-day battle—and the turning point of the war.

The second day of the battle saw fierce fighting at Little Round Top, a ridge overlooking the battlefield. Yankee riflemen from Maine held the slope against five charges by Alabama Rebels. Then, with their ammunition exhausted, the Yankees charged downhill with bayo-nets, driving the Confederates into a retreat. The following day, Lee launched Pickett's Charge, a bold attack on the center of the Union line on Cemetery Ridge, hoping to scatter the Yankees and pick them off one by one. Not only did the Confederates fail to break the Union line, but also General George Pickett lost more than half his men in the slaughter. The Union was the clear victor, and Lee's stab

SKETCH of ROUTES
of the 2nd Corps A. N. Virginia
from
Fredericksburg, Va. to Gettysburg, Pa.
and Return to
Orange C.H. Va.
JUNE 4TH TO AUGUST 1ST 1863
to accompany Report of
JED. HOTCHKISS TOP. ENG. 2nd Corps.
Prepared by Order of
LT. COL. WM. PROCTOR SMITH
Chief Engineer
A.N.V.

SCALE TEN MILES TO 1 INCH.

This map of the route to Gettysburg by Confederate map-maker Jed Hotchkiss shows roads, rivers, and mountains. Lee's decisions were shaped in large part by features of the land-scape. He moved northward between the two ranges of mountains, which provided cover for his army. A large gap in the mountains at Cashtown was the widest and most level place to cross the range. And just beyond that gap lay Gettysburg, destined by geography to become a battlefield.

TOUGH TIMES AT VICKSBURG

 When Union troops entered Vicksburg, they saw what the soldiers there had endured during the long siege—and how they tried to raise their spirits. A Northern newspaper published a document found in a Confederate camp. Written in the form of a menu from the restaurant of a fancy hotel, it took a humorous approach to the mule meat that the starving Rebels were forced to eat. Menu items included mule tail soup, mule bacon with poke greens, mule brain omelettes, hashed mule liver, and stewed side of mule (with the hair on). The "menu" also offered diners their choice of Mississippi River water or spring water, and it added, "No effort will be spared to make the visit of all as interesting as possible."

at the North had ended in defeat. To Lincoln's distress, Union commander Meade failed to pursue Lee's dejected army as it limped back into Southern territory. "We had only to stretch forth our hands and they were ours," the president mourned.

Gettysburg had cost the Confederacy 28,000 **casualties**, compared with 23,000 for the much larger Union army. To make matters worse, Confederate leaders soon learned that Vicksburg, which had held off a Union siege for nearly a year, had surrendered the day after Gettysburg, giving the North control of the Mississippi River. Some Southerners now felt doomed but kept fighting for honor's sake. One officer said, "The Confederacy totters to its destruction."

Chapter Two

TOTAL
WAR

As 1864 dawned, Union leaders formed a new plan. Keeping Confederate forces out of the North had not won the war. Now the Union would drive hard into Southern territory. Yankee soldiers would continue to battle Rebel soldiers and try to capture the Southern capital at Richmond, but now they would wage total war—burning Southern crops and farms, causing destruction and distress among **civilians** to force the South to surrender.

The North Attacks

The Union armies were now commanded by General Ulysses S. Grant, who had defended Chattanooga, Tennessee, from a Confederate attack in November 1863. In May and June of 1864, Grant launched a series of swift attacks against smaller Southern armies in Virginia. The Battle of the Wilderness, fought in thick forest near Chancellorsville, was a two-day nightmare that claimed 18,000 Union and at least 7,500 Confederate lives but did not yield a clear victory to either side. The Battle of Spotsylvania in Pennsylvania pitted 110,000 Union troops against less than half as many Rebels. The battle lasted for twelve days and saw fierce hand-to-hand combat. Never, Grant declared, had the world seen so bloody or long-lasting a conflict. In the end, the Union was victorious.

The Confederate army retreated toward Richmond. The Union army followed. They met at Cold Harbor, and 7,000 Union soldiers died in one half-hour charge. The clash ended in victory for Lee's ragged Confederate army, but many saw that the North's greater numbers and Grant's relentless attacks would eventually wear them down. One Virginia officer wrote later that "the policy of pounding had begun, and would continue until our strength should be utterly worn away."

Ulysses S. Grant proved to be the most successful of the many generals who commanded the Army of the Potomac during the war.

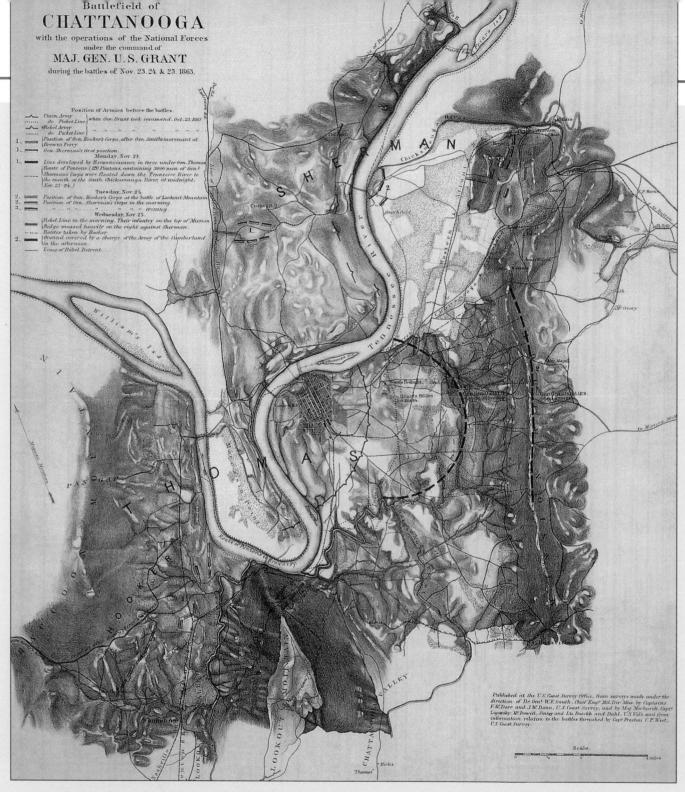

Battlefield of
CHATTANOOGA
with the operations of the National Forces
under the command of
MAJ. GEN. U.S. GRANT
during the battles of Nov. 23. 24. & 25. 1863.

Mapmakers from the U.S. Office of Coast Survey produced this map of Chattanooga, Tennessee, where Union forces commanded by Ulysses S. Grant prevented the Confederates from capturing the town. The names Hooker, Sherman, and Thomas show where Grant's officers and their men were stationed. Grant led a bold and successful attack on Confederate positions atop Mission or Missionary Ridge, the steep height overlooking the town.

Grant marched toward Petersburg, a railroad town south of Richmond. If he could seize Petersburg, he could cut off train traffic into the Confederate capital and starve it into surrender. Lee managed to rush enough troops to Petersburg to strengthen the city. Instead of a quick conquest, Grant settled in for a long siege. The Confederates holed themselves up in **trenches** and behind walls of spiked logs. The Yankees attacked again and again but could not break through. Even their clever plan to dig a tunnel under the Confederate line and blow up the defenses with gunpowder ended in failure when Union

Confederate forces built many barriers, including this mound of earth, around Petersburg, Virginia. The barriers held off the Union army for ten months, but Petersburg's defenses finally collapsed, leaving the route to the Confederate capital of Richmond unprotected.

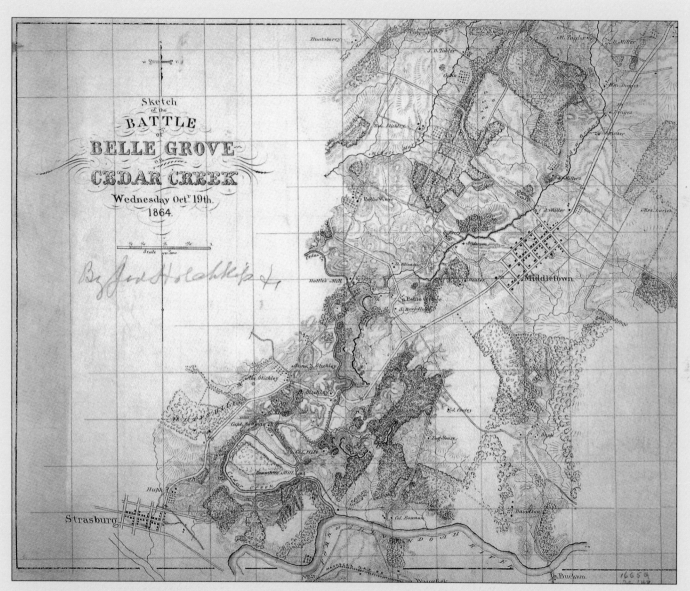

Confederate troops almost won a battle at Cedar Creek, Virginia, in October 1864. But the Union force gathered its strength and forced the Confederates to retreat. Confederate mapmaker Jed Hotchkiss, who had taken part in the battle, later made this detailed plain of the area. By the time he was working on it in February of 1865, the Confederacy was on its last legs.

troops, trapped in the crater caused by the explosion, were mowed down by Rebel soldiers on the walls. Still, Grant grimly continued the siege, certain that if he could not overcome the Confederates, he could outwait them. At the same time, he sent part of his force under General Philip H. Sheridan into Virginia's Shenandoah Valley, a fertile farmland that the Confederates had successfully defended once before. This time the Yankee troops not only kept the Rebels on the run but also burned and destroyed everything, leaving nothing to feed, shelter, or comfort enemy soldiers or civilians.

Men and Machines

The Civil War produced more than one million dead and wounded, partly because of the weapons with which it was fought. Earlier soldiers had used muskets, long guns whose barrels were smooth tubes of metal. Troops stood shoulder to shoulder and marched steadily toward the enemy. Muskets were not very accurate beyond about eighty yards, so troops began firing at that distance, then charged the enemy for hand-to-hand combat.

A new type of gun came into wide use during the Civil War. It was called the rifle, because its barrel was rifled, or engraved on the inside with spiral grooves. Rifling made the bullet spin along the barrel, which caused it to travel faster and farther than a musket ball. A rifle bullet was accurate at distances of up to 400 yards. When troops marched forward as they had done during the days of muskets, riflemen cut them down long before they got close enough for a successful charge. Another technological advance, the machine gun, fired many rounds of ammunition quickly and without reloading, although it was not widely used. Because the agricultural South produced far fewer guns and bullets than the industrial North, Confederate troops quickly learned to gather weapons and ammunition from fallen foes on the battlefield.

The new weapons made an impact, but they alone did not pile battlefields so thickly with dead and wounded that one could not ride a horse across them, as one Union officer said after Gettysburg. The real cause of the war's high casualties was the sheer number of men flung into battle again and again by both sides.

"The Hard Hand of War"

While Grant commanded the Union forces in Virginia, he sent General William T. Sherman into the heart of the South on another mission—to capture Atlanta, Georgia, an important center of Southern manufacturing and railway traffic. Its loss would cripple the Confederacy.

As Sherman pushed onward, he fought a string of battles with Confederate forces. Union losses were high, but Sherman kept going. The North had realized that its best hope of winning was to keep hurling men into battle until the

THE HEROES OF THE HUNLEY

 On the dark night of February 17, 1864, the Confederacy prepared to use a secret weapon. Nine men climbed into a 39-foot-long metal tube—one of the world's first submarines, a ship built to travel underwater. It was called the *Hunley* after Horace Hunley of New Orleans, who had paid for its construction. The nine men who boarded the *Hunley* in 1864 were truly heroic, for they knew that the first two attempts to use the submarine had ended in the deaths of the crews, including Hunley himself. With eight men turning cranks to power the *Hunley*'s propeller, the sub crept through the water toward the 207-foot-long *Housatonic*, the largest vessel of the Union navy, outside Charleston Harbor off the South Carolina coast. The *Hunley* drove a torpedo into the side of the *Housatonic*, then quickly backed away as the wooden ship exploded, burned, and sank. For the first time in history, a submarine had destroyed a battleship. But something went wrong aboard the *Hunley*, and neither the submarine nor its men made it back to shore. In 1995, the sub was found, resting on the sea bottom. The cause of its failure is still a mystery.

Artist Conrad Wise Chapman's vision of the Hunley, the submarine that the Confederates hoped would destroy the Union navy.

South ran out of soldiers. In September, Sherman's army reached Atlanta. He ordered the citizens out, set fires that spread and destroyed much of the city, and then headed toward Savannah, on the Georgia coast.

Sherman's march to the sea became a model of total war. A Southern woman named Dolly Lunt Burge described how Union soldiers descended upon her **plantation**: "[L]ike demons they rush in. My yards are full. To my

William Tecumseh Sherman, who led Union forces on a march through Georgia, had explored the area years earlier and boasted that he "knew more of Georgia than the Rebels did." This Union map shows the territory Sherman's forces covered between the city of Marietta and the Chattahoochee River. From the river, Sherman could see the great Southern city of Atlanta, which he would soon put to the torch.

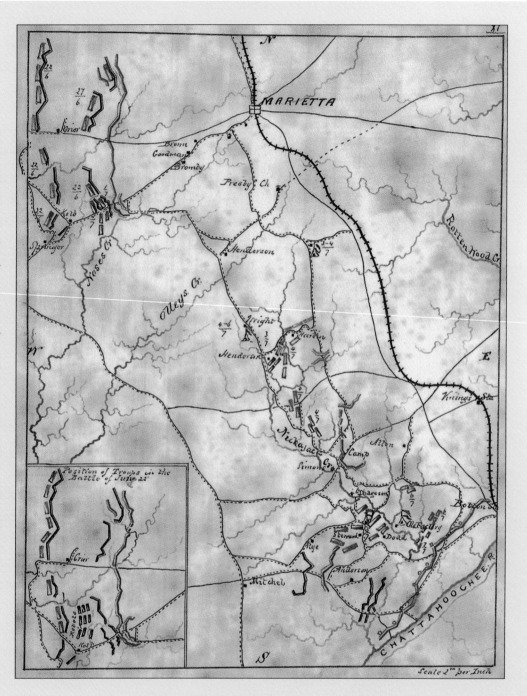

Sherman's capture of Atlanta was a sign that the end of the war was near.
By seizing and nearly destroying one of the South's main population centers, the Union
showed both its strength and its ruthlessness. The war dragged on until the following
spring, but most thoughtful observers knew that the Confederacy was doomed.

smoke house, my Dairy, Pantry, kitchen & cellar like famished wolves they come, breaking locks and whatever is in their way.... I had been repeatedly told that they would burn everything as they passed." Soldiers ripped up railways and bridges, burned crops and barns, killed livestock, and took what they wanted from the terrified and angry people. Sherman explained, "We are not only fighting hostile armies, but a hostile people, and must make old and young, rich and poor, feel the hard hand of war."

FINAL CAMPAIGNS & BATTLES

Indianapolis

Columbus

PA.

MD.

N.J.

Washington, D.C.

DEL.

ILLINOIS

INDIANA

OHIO

Wilderness
May 5-6, 1864

Spotsylvania
Court House
May 8-12, 1864

WEST
VIRGINIA

VIRGINIA

Cold Harbor
June 3, 1864

Ohio

Louisville

Richmond

Appomattox Court House
Lee surrenders to Grant
April 9, 1865

KENTUCKY

Siege of Petersburg
June 20, 1864-April 2, 1865

Nashville
Dec. 15-16, 1864

Durham

Johnston surrenders to Sherman
April 26, 1865

TENNESSEE

NORTH CAROLINA

Union
Blockade

Franklin
Nov. 30, 1864

Chattanooga

Wilmington

Kennesaw Mountain
June 27, 1864

SOUTH CAROLINA

MISS.

Columbia

Atlanta

Atlantic
Ocean

Charleston

Sherman's march
through Georgia

0   100 miles

ALABAMA

0   200 kilometers

Montgomery

© Oxford Cartographers

GEORGIA

Savannah

Mobile

Union
Blockade

Mobile Bay
Aug. 5, 1864

Jacksonville

Gulf of Mexico

FLORIDA

✸ Major battle

→ Union campaign

→ Confederate
   campaign

  Confederate state

  Union state

⛵ Union blockade

In the final months of the Civil War, Grant's Union troops occupied key positions in Virginia, trapping Lee, who had hoped to lead his men westward to continue fighting. Lee surrendered to Grant on April 9, 1865. Sherman, meanwhile, swept northward from Atlanta. Confederate general Joseph Johnston attacked Sherman several times, but finally had to surrender to him. When Union troops captured Confederate president Jefferson Davis on May 10, the war was truly over.

Lee Surrenders

By the fall of 1864, the Northern population was so disgusted with the war that Lincoln feared they would not reelect him. Some called for an end to the fighting, even if it meant Confederate independence. But the Union victories in Atlanta and the Shenandoah Valley cheered Northern voters, who reelected Lincoln.

In February 1865, Sherman led his all-devouring, all-destroying troops through South Carolina. They left Charleston—where the Civil War had started—in flames as they moved toward North Carolina and, beyond it, Richmond. In early April, Petersburg finally surrendered, leaving Richmond unprotected. President Jefferson Davis and other Confederate leaders fled their capital, which was in Union hands on April 3. Lincoln visited the fallen Southern stronghold, where African-American former slaves hailed him with thanks and prayers as their liberator.

Lee's army was still in the field, but Sherman was approaching from the south while Grant approached from the north. Lee tried to retreat westward but was cut off and surrounded by Union forces that numbered 115,000 to his 30,000. Knowing that defeat was unavoidable, the Confederate commander surrendered to Grant in a town called Appomattox Court House in Virginia on April 9. Although a few Southern leaders and troops continued to

Robert E. Lee (right), perhaps the most skilled and respected military commander of the Civil War, surrenders to Union commander Ulysses S. Grant in a painting titled **Let Us Have Peace.**

fight for another month or so, the war ended at Appomattox. Lee wrote a farewell to his troops, praising them for their courage and telling them that there was no shame in yielding to "overwhelming numbers and resources." And Grant later wrote, "I felt like anything rather than rejoicing at the downfall of a foe who had fought so long and valiantly, and had suffered so much."

Chapter Three

REBUILDING A NATION

The Civil War proved that the federal government was stronger than states' rights. The issue of secession had been settled once and for all. The war had also succeeded in freeing the African-American slaves. Now how would the United States move forward, when the North viewed the South as a captive enemy and the South saw the North as a cruel tyrant? In his second inaugural address in March 1865, with Union victory close at hand, Lincoln had spoken of the need to "bind up the nation's wounds." Healing those

Ill and elderly former slaves gather to receive food distributed by the Freedmen's Bureau. The federal government organized the bureau because it realized that African Americans would need help in making the shift from slaves to free citizens. The bureau made important progress in providing education to African Americans. By 1870, it had established about four thousand schools for black children in the South. Half of the teachers were free African Americans from the North.

wounds would be a task almost as difficult, in its way, as winning the war had been.

Plans for Reconstruction

Even before the end of the war, leaders in the North had debated how to draw the South back into the Union. They put forward plans for the reconstruction, or rebuilding, of the South. President Lincoln did not want to punish or humiliate the South. His idea was that any state that had seceded could rejoin the Union when 10 percent of its voters swore loyalty to the federal government. Southerners could govern their own states, although they would have to outlaw slavery, and former Confederate soldiers would have the rights of

DEATH OF A WAR CRIMINAL

 The war's end meant that captured soldiers who had been held as prisoners of war could return home. Captives on both sides had endured vile conditions or had perished by the tens of thousands. The worst conditions and the most deaths, however, were at Andersonville prison in Georgia, where as many as 30,000 Union soldiers were held at the same time. Thirst, starvation, disease, and brutality claimed the lives of nearly a third of all prisoners during the final year of the war. Stories and photographs made the Northern public aware of the misery at Andersonville and led to the trial of Henry Wirz, the prison's commander. Wirz was hanged in November 1865, the only Confederate officer to pay with his life for war crimes.

Henry Wirz, commander of a dreadful prisoner-of-war camp in Georgia, was hanged in November 1865 for his crimes. Matthew Brady, a photographer who produced many memorable Civil War images, photographed the execution.

The assassination of President Lincoln less than a week after Lee's surrender was a tragedy for both North and South. The North lost the capable president who had guided it to victory. The South lost a president who had made thoughtful and humane plans for bringing the defeated enemy back into the Union.

other citizens. Republicans in Congress, however, favored a harsher plan that required loyalty oaths from half of all voters before a state could rejoin the Union. It also banned former Confederates from voting or holding office.

Congress and the president agreed, however, on the need to help the black freedmen, or former slaves, find their place in the new society. In 1865, the federal government created the Freedmen's Bureau. This government agency, originally a branch of the army, set up schools for Southern blacks, helped freedmen get land, and offered food, medical aid, and clothing to those in need.

The President Is Slain

The president and Congress never did reach a compromise on Reconstruction. On April 14, less than a week after the war ended, Southern sympathizer John Wilkes Booth assassinated Lincoln with what some people called "the last shot of the war." The tragedy hardened the hearts of many Northerners against the South. New Yorker George Templeton Strong wrote in his diary, "People who pitied our misguided brethren yesterday, and thought they had been punished enough already...talk approvingly today of...judges, juries, gaolers [jailers], and hangmen...."

Vice President Andrew Johnson of Tennessee, the only Southern senator who had stayed loyal to the Union, became president after Lincoln's death. Although Johnson claimed to follow Lincoln's wishes, he lacked Lincoln's imagination, popular support, and ability to communicate. Johnson's plan for Reconstruction outlawed slavery but limited voting rights to whites and let individual Southern states decide how to treat their newly freed blacks. Congress, feeling that Johnson's plan was too soft on white Southerners and too hard on African-American ones, refused to accept it.

Who Will Control the South?

In the fight for control of Reconstruction, Johnson was doomed to lose. Opponents in Congress overruled him and nearly succeeded in getting him thrown out of the White House in 1868. In the end, Congress set the **federal** Reconstruction policies, but the Northern Reconstructionists found themselves battling plantation owners, former Confederates, and other Southerners, who may have been beaten but who were not ready to give up

Andrew Johnson became president after Lincoln's death, but he lacked Lincoln's power and popularity. In 1868, he was accused of misusing his authority and impeached, or forced to stand trial in the Senate. Johnson managed to remain in office, but he was unable to carry out Lincoln's plans for Reconstruction in the South.

control of their region.

The Civil War had ended slavery, but it had not erased racism, the belief held by many whites that black people were inferior to them

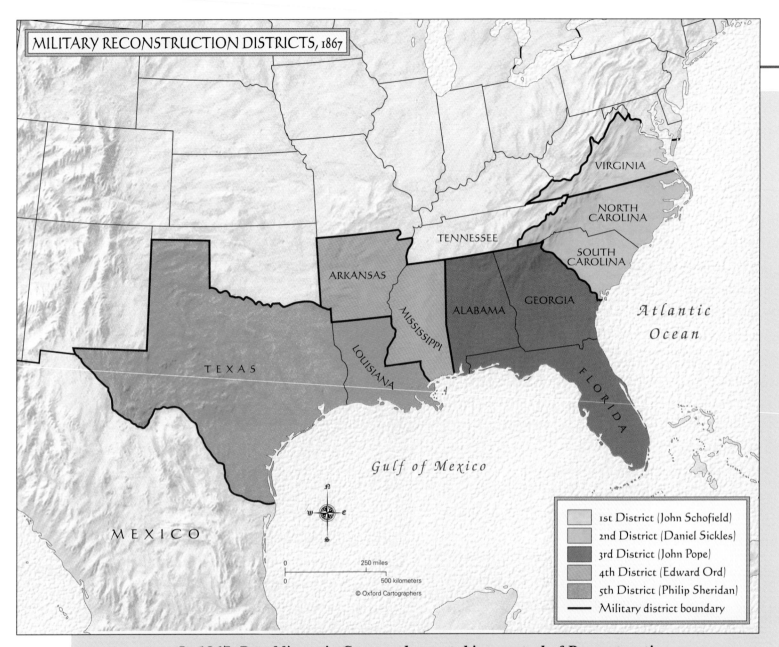

VIRGINIA

NORTH CAROLINA

TENNESSEE

SOUTH CAROLINA

ARKANSAS

Atlantic Ocean

MISSISSIPPI

ALABAMA

GEORGIA

LOUISIANA

TEXAS

FLORIDA

Gulf of Mexico

MEXICO

1st District (John Schofield)
2nd District (Daniel Sickles)
3rd District (John Pope)
4th District (Edward Ord)
5th District (Philip Sheridan)
Military district boundary

0   250 miles
0   500 kilometers

© Oxford Cartographers

*In 1867, Republicans in Congress began taking control of Reconstruction.
One of their first acts was to divide the South into military districts, each governed
by a military commander. The commanders were officers, such as Philip Sheridan, who
had waged war against the South just a few years earlier. Some people who had hoped
for a gentler Reconstruction saw the military districts as a continuation of the war,
but the districts lasted only a few years, until the states reentered the Union.*

and should not have equal rights. Southern whites resented Reconstruction policies aimed at educating blacks and increasing social equality. They also deeply resented the Northern governors, administrators, and merchants, who flocked into the region for jobs or business opportunities. Southerners called these unwelcome newcomers carpetbaggers because they often carried suitcases made of carpet material. To the devastated Southerners, they were vultures feeding on the suffering of the Confederacy. Those Southerners who cooperated with the carpetbaggers were scornfully called scalawags.

Reconstruction became a long drawn-out struggle. Northerners, including **abolitionists**, tried to make the South what they thought it should be—and, in some cases, to punish it. White Southerners, meanwhile, stubbornly and sullenly clung to the scraps of their former social and racial system—for example, by bullying black people into calling them "master." Caught in the middle were the Southern blacks, who had no property of their own. Many went to work for their former owners because they had no other way to earn a living.

Black Codes and Civil Rights

In 1865 and 1866, some Southern states passed new laws called Black Codes to control free black people. Among other things, the codes required blacks to work for whites to pay off

Tragically for all Americans, the end of the war and of slavery did not bring an end to racial prejudice and violence. The Ku Klux Klan, whose costume included white hood, was only one of many white groups that made life difficult for blacks after the war.

debts or as punishment for being unemployed or homeless. Congress had ended slavery for good with the Thirteenth Amendment to the Constitution in January 1865, before the war ended, but during Reconstruction some Southern blacks found themselves in circumstances that felt very much like slavery.

The Black Codes were not the only tool that racist Southern whites used to keep African Americans from claiming their new place in society. Some whites formed secret societies dedicated to terrorizing blacks, destroying their schools and homes, and even killing them. The most feared and violent group was the Ku Klux Klan, founded in 1866. Its burnings and murders so outraged Northerners that, in 1867, Congress tightened its control over the South, sending military commanders and troops to oversee the region and allowing African Americans to vote in state elections. This infuriated Southerners and made them even more determined to resist—and the vicious cycle continued.

Congress took several other steps to protect the rights of African Americans in the South. In 1866, it gave additional resources to the Freedmen's Bureau. It passed the Civil Rights Act, which made African Americans full citizens and gave the federal government power to overturn unjust state laws such as the Black Codes. The Fourteenth Amendment to the Constitution, also passed in 1866, was a more permanent version of the Civil Rights Act, giving African-American citizens "equal protection under the law." Yet these measures did not allow blacks to vote in federal elections. Not until the Fifteenth Amendment in 1869 were African-American men guaranteed the right to vote.

(Women could not yet vote, no matter what their race.) African-American voters helped Republicans win power in local and state elections in the South. Blacks also began holding

General James Garfield was a staunch supporter of the Freedmen's Bureau. He said, "Now, that we have made them free, we will stand by these black allies! We will stand by them until the sun of liberty shall shine with equal ray upon every man, black or white, throughout the union."

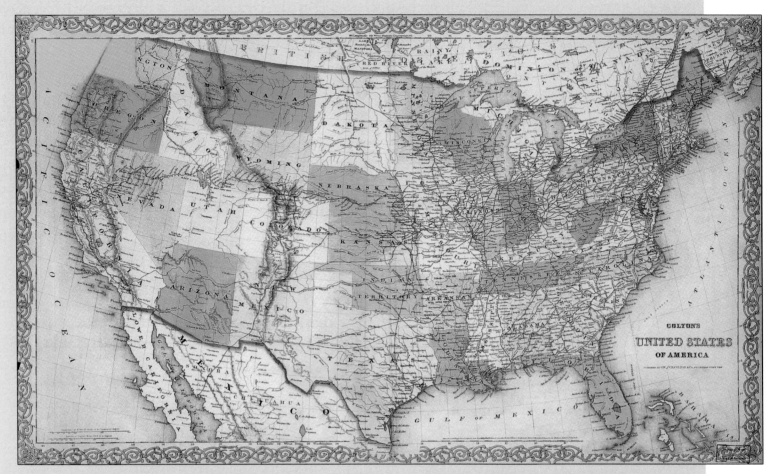

George Colton's 1869 map of the United States would have looked quite different if the Southern states had succeeded in forming a separate nation. Instead, the map shows that the country is not only whole, but growing. New railroads push westward, and the western territories are becoming states.

office in both state legislatures and Congress.

The End of Reconstruction

Reconstruction changed the laws of the South, but it failed to change many hearts and minds.

The Ku Klux Klan did not disappear. Some white Southerners continued to threaten and abuse black people, or simply refused to give them jobs or rent them land or housing. "Wherever I go," wrote a white Missourian traveling through the

South, "...I hear people talk in such a way as to indicate they are yet unable to conceive of the Negro as possessing any rights at all."

Ulysses S. Grant, commander of the victorious Union army, was president for two terms after Johnson. His presidency from 1868 to 1876 was filled with scandal, **corruption**, and an economic depression. As a result, the Republicans began losing power. The Democrats—and the white Southern voters who supported them—gained strength. At the same time Northern interest in the South was fading, after fifteen years of war and Reconstruction. The election of 1876 was a close contest between Republican Rutherford B. Hayes and Democrat Samuel Tilden. Arguments over the accuracy of vote counts in three Southern states made it impossible to declare a winner until early in 1877, when Democrats and Republicans in Congress made a deal. Southern Democrats agreed to accept Hayes as president, and Northern Republicans agreed to end the military occupation of the South and let black and white Southerners work out their own fates.

Reconstruction was over. Yet the healing that Lincoln had envisioned was far from complete. The painful legacy of the Civil War, of Reconstruction, and of the battle over African-American rights remains alive in the United States a century and a half later. At the dawn of the twenty-first century, people still argue about what the Confederate flag symbolizes—a proud region's gallant heritage...or slavery and racism?

Glossary

abolitionist: one who works to abolish, or end, slavery

bayonet: stabbing blade attached to a rifle and used for hand-to-hand combat

besiege: to hold under siege, a military tactic in which a city or fort is surrounded to prevent its defenders from escaping or receiving aid and supplies

border states: slave states along the border between the North and the South that remained loyal to the Union

casualty: loss of a soldier to death, injury, or capture

civilian: ordinary citizen, someone not a member of a military force

corruption: dishonesty or illegal dealings

desert: to leave military duty without permission, usually considered a serious crime under military law

federal: relating to the national government

inaugural: relating to an inauguration, the formal start of a term of office

johnnycake: type of bread made with cornmeal, often cooked in a frying pan over a campfire

parley: brief truce for communication between opposing sides

plantation: large farm devoted to production of a single crop, usually for sale rather than for local use

prejudice: dislike or unfair treatment based on race

secede: to formally leave or withdraw from

segregated: separated by race

trench: ditch or tunnel used as a defensive position by troops, sometimes for long periods

Map List

ABOUT THE HISTORICAL MAPS

The historical maps used in this book are primary source documents found in the Library of Congress Map Division. You will find these maps on pages : 9, 15, 18, 23, 25, 28, 41.

Chronology

1863 January 1: The Emancipation Proclamation frees the Southern slaves.
May 2–4: Robert E. Lee's Confederate forces win a victory at Chancellorsville.
July 1–3: The Battle of Gettysburg ends Lee's hopes of advancing into Northern territory.
July 4: A Confederate army surrenders to Union forces at Vicksburg. December 8:
President Lincoln announces a plan for reconstruction of the Union after the war.

1864 July 2: The U.S. Congress passes a reconstruction plan more severe than Lincoln's.
November 8: The Union reelects Lincoln to the presidency. November 15: Union
general William T. Sherman begins a destructive march through Georgia.

1865 January: Congress passes the Thirteenth Amendment, abolishing slavery throughout
the United States. March 3: Congress creates the Freedmen's Bureau to assist former
slaves. April 3: Union forces take Richmond, Virginia, the Confederate capital.
April 9: Lee surrenders to Union leader General Ulysses S. Grant, ending the war.
April 14: Confederate sympathizer John Wilkes Booth assassinates Lincoln.

1866 Congress passes the Civil Rights Act, making black Americans citizens, and passes
the Fourteenth Amendment to guarantee equal legal standing to all citizens.
The Ku Klux Klan starts terrorizing African Americans and promoting white power.

1869 Congress passes the Fifteenth Amendment, granting former slaves the right to vote.

1877 Republican Rutherford B. Hayes takes office after a disputed election, the last U.S.
troops leave the South, and Reconstruction ends.

Further Reading

Catton, Bruce. *The American Heritage New History of the Civil War.* New York: Viking, 1996.

Clinton, Catherine. *Scholastic Encyclopedia of the Civil War.* New York: Scholastic Reference, 1999.

Dolan, Edward. *The American Civil War: A House Divided.* Brookfield, CT: Millbrook, 1997.

Dudley, William, ed. *The Civil War: Opposing Viewpoints.* San Diego: Greenhaven Press, 1995.

Gay, Kathleen. *Civil War.* New York: Twenty-First Century Books, 1995.

Grabowski, Patricia. *Robert E. Lee: Confederate General.* New York: Chelsea House, 2001.

Hakim, Joy. *War, Terrible War.* New York: Oxford University Press, 1999.

Hewson, Martha. *Stonewall Jackson: Confederate General.* Philadelphia: Chelsea House, 2001.

Janis, Herbert. *The Civil War for Kids: A History with 21 Activities.* Chicago: Chicago Review Press, 1999.

McElfresh, Earl. *Maps and Mapmakers of the Civil War.* New York: Abrams, 1999.

Meltzer, Milton, ed. *Voices from the Civil War: A Documentary History of the Great American Conflict.* New York: Crowell, 1989.

Otfinoski, Steven. *John Wilkes Booth and the Civil War.* Woodbridge, CT: Blackbirch Press, 1999.

Pflueger, Lynda. *Jeb Stuart: Confederate Cavalry General.* Springfield, NJ: Enslow, 1998.

Piggins, Carol Ann. *A Multicultural Portrait of the Civil War.* North Bellmore, NY: Marshall Cavendish, 1994.

Ransom, Candice F. *Children of the Civil War.* Minneapolis: Carolrhoda Books, 1998.

Remstein, Henna. *William Sherman: Union General.* New York: Chelsea House, 2001.

Seidman, Rachel F. *The Civil War: A History in Documents.* New York: Oxford University Press, 2001.

Stanchak, John E. *Visual Dictionary of the Civil War.*
New York: Dorling Kindersley, 2000.

Sullivan, George. *Mathew Brady: His Life and Work.*
New York: Cobblehill Books, 1994.

Time-Life Books. *Brother Against Brother: Time-Life Books History of the Civil War.* New York: Prentice-Hall Press, 1990.

WEBSITES

www.homepages/dsu.edu/jankej/civilwar/civilwar.htm
(Civil War Index Page, maintained by Dakota State University, is a collection of links to on-line resources in dozens of categories)

www.sunsite.utk.edu/civil-war/warweb.html
(American Civil War Homepage, maintained by the University of Tennessee, is an award-winning educational site with links to hundreds of on-line sources)

www.americancivilwar.com
(American Civil War Website includes time lines, battle maps, documents such as the Emancipation Proclamation, biographies of key figures, reading lists, and links to other on-line sources)

ABOUT THE AUTHOR

Rebecca Stefoff is the author of many nonfiction books for children and young adults. In Marshall Cavendish's North American Historical Atlases, she draws upon her interests in historical maps, life in different eras, and military campaigns to tell the story of key events in American history. This volume is the companion to *The Civil War: 1861–1863*, in which she wrote about the first half of the war. Stefoff lives in Oregon, far from the scenes of the Civil War, but she has visited many Civil War sites. She appreciates the efforts of the National Park Service, state and local historical societies, and other groups that work to preserve sites and relics of the war so that they may continue to educate and inspire us.

Index

Entries are filed letter-by-letter. Page numbers for illustrations and maps are in **boldface**.